# CHRISTMAS

# Ode to the King

Daniel de Eagle

Copyright © 2023 Daniel de Eagle

All rights reserved.

The content contained within this book may not be reproduced, duplicated, or transmitted in any form or retrieval system now known or to be invented without direct written permission from the author or publisher. Under no circumstances will any blame or legal responsibility be held against the publisher, or author, for any damages, reparation, or monetary loss due to the information contained within this book. Either directly or indirectly.

EBOOK ISBN: 978-969-3992-60-1

PAPERBACK ISBN: 978-969-3992-61-8

HARDBACK ISBN: 978-969-3992-62-5

Library of Congress Control Number: 2015904837

Daniel de Eagle, Euless , TX

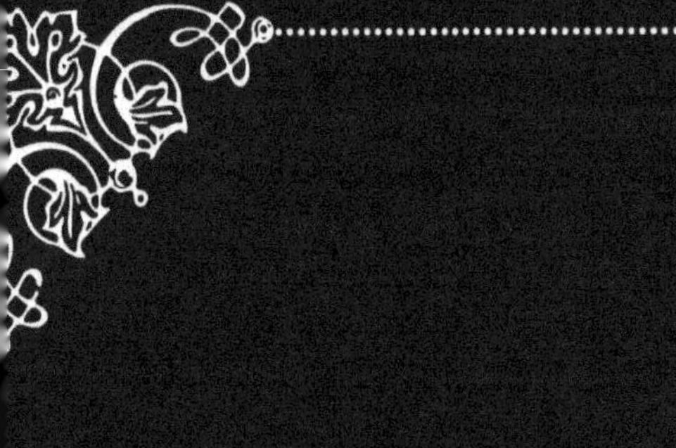

# Table of Contents

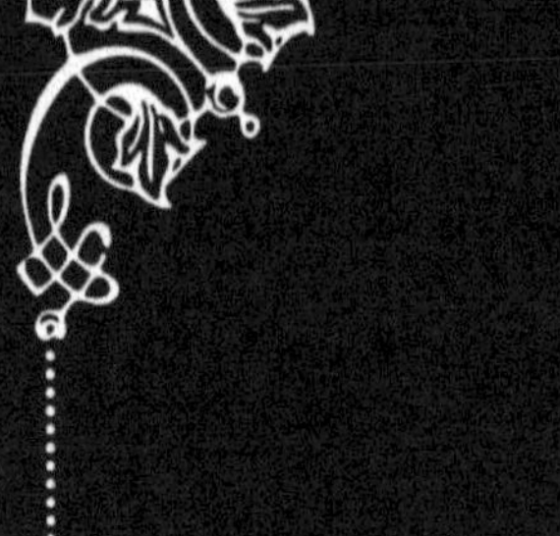

# Dedication

This heartfelt dedication is for the future generations who will encounter the rich tapestry of Christmas traditions. It is also extended to those among us who, in the present, may find themselves unaware of the origins and true essence of this cherished celebration. Furthermore, this dedication is offered to the poets and creatives who skillfully weave enchanting images through their mastery of words and artistry. May this book, "Christmas Ode to the King," serve as a guiding light, illuminating the path to understanding and appreciation for all who delve into its pages.

# About Daniel de Eagle

Daniel de Eagle is a dedicated servant leader and prayer missionary from the Generation X timeline. He serves as the co-ministry leader of Covering Eagle Ministries alongside Minister Nikki his spouse. Daniel also serves as Lead Prayer Strategist and Trainer at When Eagles Pray Trainer (W.E.P.T.), an arm of CEM that provides strategic online and in-person prayer resources to the local and global Body of Christ.

With a remarkable 39 years of active involvement in the prayer ministry, Daniel is known for his strong flow in prophetic intercession and his ability to offer deep yet simplistic teaching insights on all aspects of prayer, catering to individuals at various levels of Christian maturity. He firmly believes that prayer is from the heart and about producing tangible results, as inspired by James 5:16.

Throughout his journey, Daniel has served on the leadership teams of numerous church-led and ancillary ministry-led prayer initiatives across Europe, Africa, and North America. He currently serves as a Governmental Level Intercessor for certain nations while personally providing prayer coverage to global Church Leaders.

Daniel's passions extend to marriage and family, prayer, and the marketplace. In 1997, he completed his Diploma in Christian Ministries program with a focus on Youth and Community development at CICM, UK. Additionally, he holds an Associate Degree in International Business and Trade, as well as a Bachelor's degree in Business Administration with a specialization in Small Business Management.

For the past 26 years, Daniel has been happily married to his wife and ministry partner, Nikki. Together, they cohost the annual Marriage Reignited Gala event, which celebrates and strengthens the marriages of heterosexual couples.

To connect with Daniel and stay updated on his work, you can follow him on Twitter @daniel_de_eagle, Instagram as daniel_de_eagle, find his YouTube channel under the name Daniel de Eagle, and locate him on Facebook as Daniel de Eagle. His inspirational quotes can also be found on the Facebook Page "Prayer Quotes and Reflections". He can also be found on TikTok under the username @daniel_de_eagle.

In the words of Daniel himself, "I'm not esoteric but I spit lyrics as a timeless psychedelic cleric on the Word hallucinogenic with a unique homiletic style." This quote captures the essence of his personality and resonates with present-day and tech-savvy generations.

# About The Book

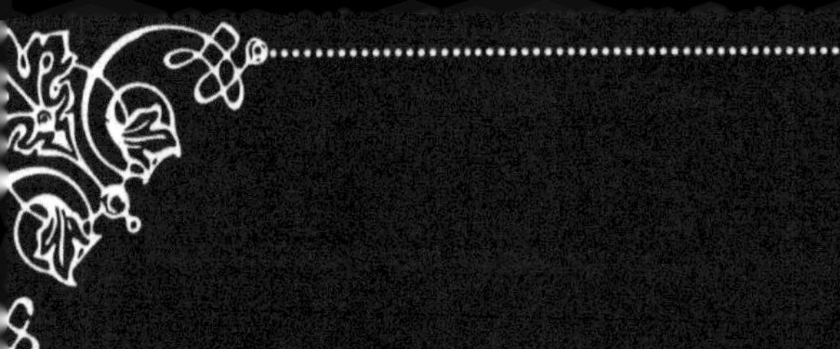

" In "Christmas Ode to the King", I embark on a poetic quest to revive what has been lost in translation. The passing down of messages from one generation to another is vulnerable to the perils of misinterpretation. My fervent desire is to illuminate the world with the profound significance that lies within every Christmas tradition. By unraveling the true essence of these cherished customs, we can cultivate a deeper appreciation and understanding of the blessings bestowed upon us during this sacred season. Let us embrace the power of clarity, for it is through this unobscured lens that we truly grasp the beauty and meaning that permeate our festive celebrations.

# Ode 1.

# Reflecting on His Birth, Death, and Resurrection.

*Oh, King divine, born in humble manger's embrace,*

*In this season of joy, we celebrate your grace.*

*A tale of birth, death, and resurrection untold,*

*A story of love, redemption, and miracles unfold.*


*In Bethlehem's stable, a star shone so bright,*

*Guiding shepherds and wise men through the night.*

*Born of a virgin, a miracle so grand,*

*You, the King of kings, came to save our land.*

*Your birth, a symbol of hope and peace,*

*A gift to mankind, a divine release.*

*Wrapped in swaddling clothes, so meek and mild,*

*You, the Savior, came to reconcile.*


*Yet, your journey did not end in that humble stall,*

*For you were destined to answer a greater call.*

*A life of sacrifice, love, and boundless grace,*

*Leading us to a higher, eternal place.*

*On a cross, you bore our sins and our strife,*

*Nailed to the wood, giving us eternal life.*

*Your death, a testament to your selfless love,*

*A sacrifice so great, descending from above.*


*But death could not hold you, O King of all,*

*For you rose victorious, breaking sin's thrall.*

*Resurrected, triumphant, you conquered the grave,*

*Offering salvation to all who would crave.*

*So, as we gather 'round the Christmas tree,*

*Let us remember the true reason to be free.*

*Not just the gifts and merriment we share,*

*But the birth, death, and resurrection we declare.*

*Oh, King divine, at this Christmas season,*

*We honor your birth, your death, and resurrection.*

*May your love and light forever shine,*

*Guiding us through life's journey, divine.*

In your presence, we find hope and peace,

A love that will never cease.

Oh, King of kings, we bow before your throne,

Forever grateful, your children, your own.

# Record Your Observations

# Ode 2.

# Reflecting on Family Gatherings at Christmas.

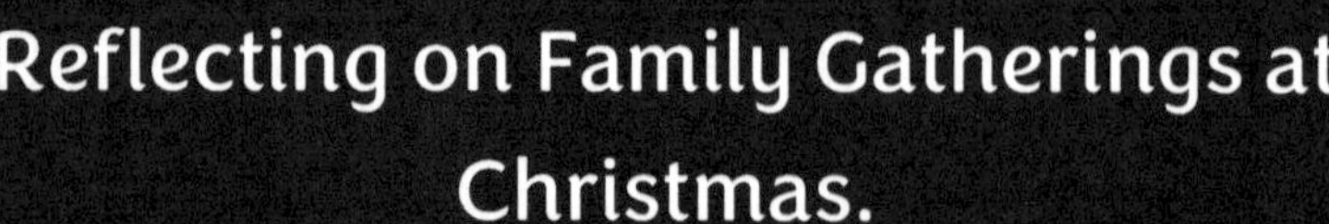

*Oh, King of Kings, we gather near,*

*With loved ones close, our hearts sincere.*

*In this season of joy and cheer,*

*We celebrate your birth, oh King so dear.*


*Family gatherings, a cherished delight,*

*As we come together, hearts shining bright.*

*From far and wide, we journey near,*

*To share in love, this time of the year.*

*Around the table, we gather 'round,*

*Laughter and stories, a joyful sound.*

*The aroma of feasts fills the air,*

*As we savor the blessings that we share.*

*In the warmth of love, we find our peace,*

*A bond that strengthens, it will not cease.*

*Through ups and downs, we stand as one,*

*United by love, under the Christmas sun.*

*Oh, King at Christmas, we honor you,*

*For the gift of family, so precious and true.*

*Through your birth, you've shown us the way,*

*To love, to forgive, to cherish each day.*


*As we gather, we remember your grace,*

*A love that transcends time and space.*

*In our family gatherings, we see your light,*

*Guiding us through the darkest night.*

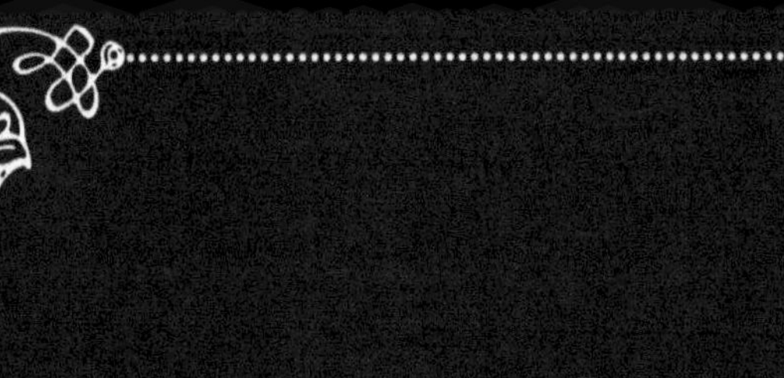

*So, King of Kings, we raise our voice,*

*In gratitude, we rejoice.*

*For family gatherings, a gift so grand,*

*A testament to your loving hand.*

*In this season of love and cheer,*

*We celebrate your birth, oh King so dear.*

*May our family gatherings always be,*

*A reflection of your love for eternity.*

# Record your observations.

# Ode 3.

# Reflecting on the Nativity Scene.

*Oh, King of kings, we gather 'round,*

*To honor your birth on hallowed ground.*

*In humble manger, you came to earth,*

*A gift of love, of infinite worth.*


*The Nativity Scene, a sacred sight,*

*Brings joy and wonder on this holy night.*

*Mary and Joseph, with hearts aglow,*

*Watch over baby Jesus, our hearts bestow.*

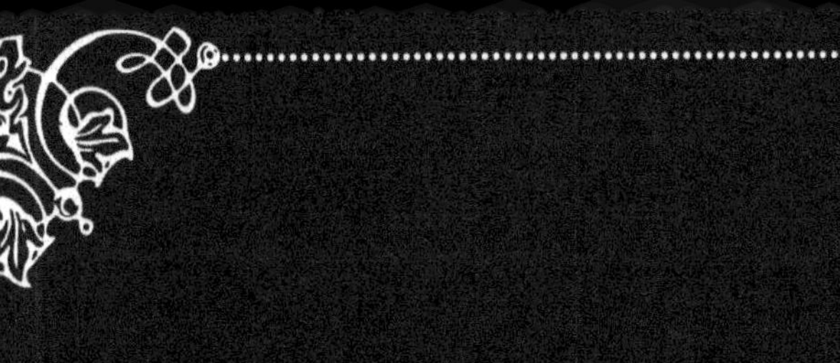

In Bethlehem's stable, a humble place,

The Son of God, adorned with grace.

Surrounded by shepherds, lowly and meek,

They kneel in reverence, their faith they speak.


Angels above, with voices so clear,

Sing of your glory, for all to hear.

Their heavenly chorus, a symphony divine,

Proclaims your arrival, a sign so fine.

*The Wise Men, guided by a star so bright,*

*Bring gifts of gold, frankincense, and myrrh in sight.*

*They journey from afar, with hearts aflame,*

*To honor your majesty, in your holy name.*




*Oh, King at Christmas, you bring us hope,*

*In your presence, our souls elope.*

*Through the Nativity Scene, we behold,*

*The miracle of your birth, a story untold.*

As we gather 'round, with loved ones near,

We cherish the blessings that Christmas brings here.

In the Nativity Scene, we find solace and peace,

A reminder of your love that will never cease.

So, let us rejoice, with hearts full of cheer,

As we celebrate your birth, this time of year.

Oh, King at Christmas, our hearts we raise,

In gratitude and awe, forever we praise.

# Record your observations.

# Ode 4.

# Reflecting on Christmas Decorations.

*Oh, King of kings, in this season of cheer,*

*We gather 'round, your presence drawing near.*

*Amidst the decorations, symbols so bright,*

*We find the meaning, the essence of your light.*


*The Christmas tree, adorned with care,*

*An evergreen reminder, steadfast and fair.*

*Its branches reaching, pointing to the sky,*

*A symbol of eternal life, never to die.*

*Lights twinkling, casting a warm glow,*

*They speak of your radiance, a heavenly show.*

*In the darkest of nights, they brightly shine,*

*Guiding us to your love, so divine.*


*Ornaments hanging, each with its own tale,*

*Angels, stars, and bells, they never fail,*

*To tell the story of your birth, so grand,*

*And the beauty of creation, crafted by your hand.*

*Wreaths, in circles, their message profound,*

*Eternity's embrace, forever to be found.*

*With evergreen leaves, they symbolize your love,*

*Endless and unchanging, from heaven above.*


*Holly and ivy, intertwined and strong,*

*They speak of faithfulness, an eternal song.*

*Holly's red berries, a reminder of your sacrifice,*

*And ivy's steadfastness, a symbol of life's ties.*

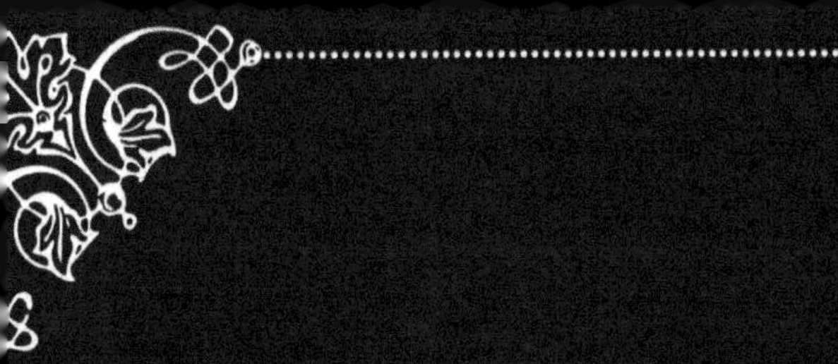

The Nativity Scene, a tableau of grace,

Mary, Joseph, baby Jesus, in that sacred place.

Shepherds and Wise Men, their homage paid,

A reminder of your birth, the foundation laid.


Stars shining bright, like the one of old,

Guiding the Wise Men, their story untold.

They symbolize your light, leading the way,

To the humble manger, where you lay.

*Candles flickering, their flames aglow,*

*They represent your presence, a warmth to bestow.*

*In their gentle light, we find solace and peace,*

*A reminder of your love, that will never cease.*

*Red and green, colors of Christmas attire,*

*They hold deep symbolism, setting hearts on fire.*

*Red, for your blood, shed for our sake,*

*Green, for life and renewal, your love to partake.*

Bells ringing, their joyful sound,

Announcing your birth, all around.

They fill the air with celebration and glee,

A chorus of praise, for all to see.


Oh, King of kings, as we decorate and adorn,

We honor your presence, on this Christmas morn.

In each decoration, we find your love and grace,

A reflection of your glory, in this sacred space.

*So, let us rejoice, as we gather near,*

*In the beauty of decorations, so clear.*

*Oh, King of kings, we sing your praise,*

*In this season of joy, our voices we raise.*

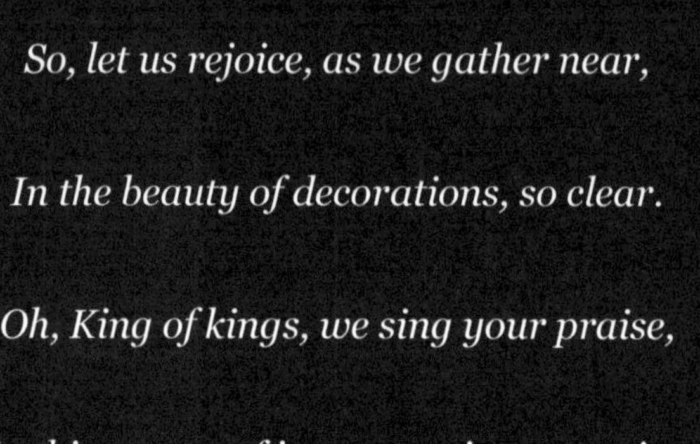

# Record your observations.

# Ode 5.

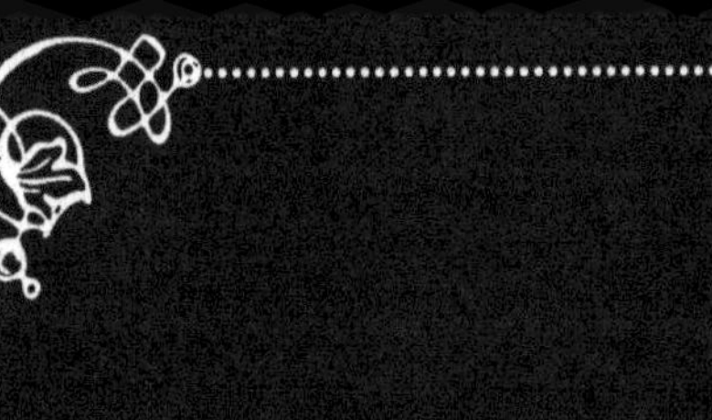

# Reflecting on Christmas Gifts.

*Oh, King of kings, in this season of cheer,*

*We gather 'round, your presence drawing near.*

*Amidst the gifts exchanged, a symbol so bright,*

*We find the essence of your love, shining with light.*


*Gifts given at Christmas, a gesture so grand,*

*Reflecting your generosity, spreading across the land.*

*In each present wrapped with care and delight,*

*We see your love, shining through the night.*

*The act of giving, a symbol of love's embrace,*

*Expressing gratitude, extending grace.*

*Just as you, oh King, were given to us all,*

*We give gifts to honor, to answer love's call.*

*Each gift bestowed holds a meaning so dear,*

*A token of affection, bringing joy and cheer.*

*Symbols of friendship, peace, and hope,*

*Through gifts, our love and connection elope.*

*Mirroring the Wise Men, who traveled afar,*

*Bearing gifts fit for a king, guided by a star.*

*We too, present treasures, with hearts aglow,*

*In reverence and honor, to you, our love we show.*

*Gifts shared in abundance, a reflection of your grace,*

*We recognize our blessings, as we embrace.*

*Through giving, we share, with those in need,*

*Extending your love, through every generous deed.*

*Gifts strengthen relationships, building a bond,*

*A language of love, beyond words, beyond beyond.*

*Thoughtfulness and care, wrapped in each present,*

*Expressing our love, a sentiment so pleasant.*


*The surprise and delight, as gifts are unveiled,*

*Bringing laughter and joy, as stories are regaled.*

*In each moment, a glimpse of your love we find,*

*As hearts are warmed, and spirits are aligned.*

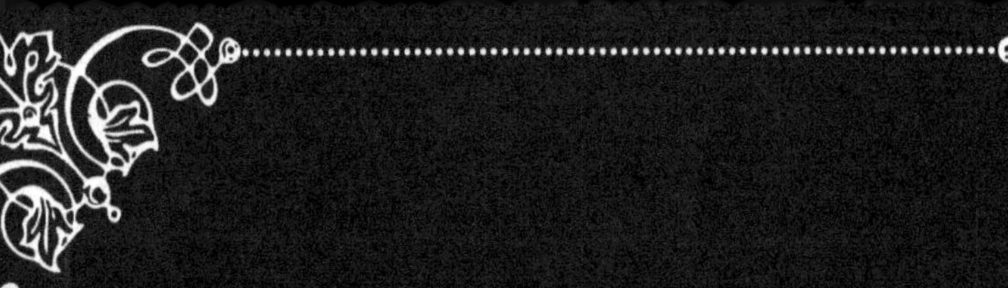

*Oh, King of kings, as we give and receive,*

*May our gifts reflect your love, and never deceive.*

*In each present exchanged, may your presence be known,*

*A reminder of your love, forever to be shown.*

*So, let us rejoice, as we gather near,*

*In the beauty of gifts, so sincere.*

*Oh, King of kings, we sing your praise,*

*In this season of giving, our voices we raise.*

# Record your observations.

# Ode 6.

# Reflecting on Christmas Carols.

*Oh, King of kings, in this season of love,*

*We gather 'round, our voices rise above.*

*With hearts united, we join in song,*

*To celebrate your birth, our voices strong.*

*Carol singing, a cherished tradition we hold,*

*A symphony of praise, a story being told.*

*In melodies sweet, we proclaim your grace,*

*Filling the air, as we seek your embrace.*

*Through carols old and carols new,*

*We honor your birth, our love we renew.*

*Each verse and chorus, a testament true,*

*To the joy and hope that in you we pursue.*


*From humble manger to starlit sky,*

*The carols resound, as angels on high.*

*They sang of your glory, the good news they brought,*

*A Savior is born, our redemption is sought.*

*In the frosty air, our breath visible,*

*We sing of your love, so tangible.*

*Voices united, in harmony we blend,*

*A chorus of faith, that will never end.*


*Oh, how the carols fill our hearts with cheer,*

*As we sing of your love, so pure and clear.*

*In each note sung, we find peace and light,*

*Guiding us through darkness, shining so bright.*

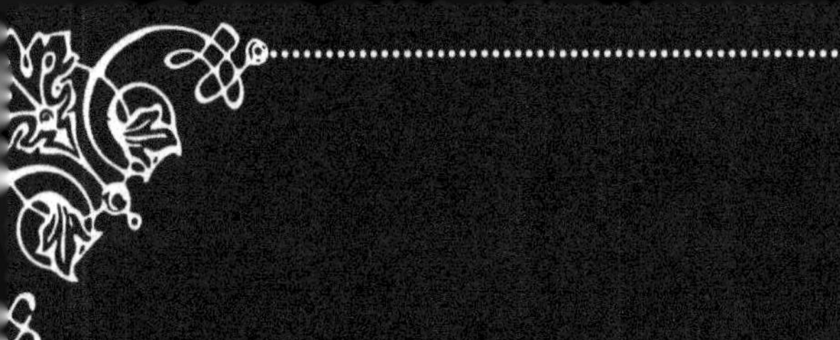

*The carols speak of your humble birth,*

*Of shepherds and Wise Men, who traveled the earth.*

*They tell of your love, that knows no bounds,*

*A love that in our hearts forever resounds.*


*Through carol singing, we share the joy,*

*Of your arrival, as a baby boy.*

*We lift our voices, in worship and praise,*

*Proclaiming your name, in endless ways.*

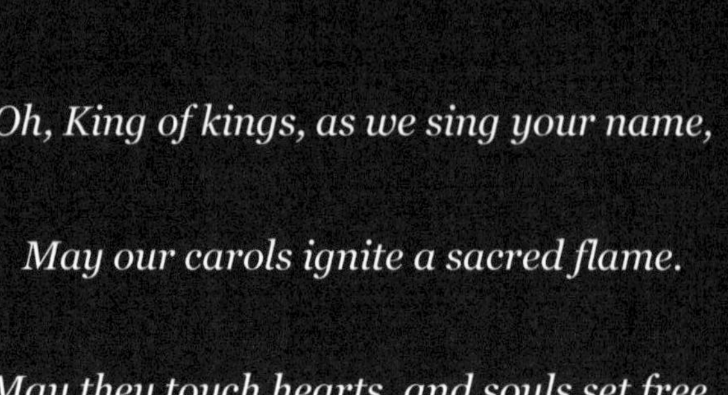

Oh, King of kings, as we sing your name,

May our carols ignite a sacred flame.

May they touch hearts, and souls set free,

Spreading your love, for all to see.



So, let us rejoice, as we gather near,

In the beauty of carols, so dear.

Oh, King of kings, we sing your praise,

In this season of joy, our voices we raise.

# Record your observations.

# Ode 7.

# Reflecting on Church Services at Christmas

*Oh, King of kings, in this season of grace,*

*We gather in your house, seeking your embrace.*

*In church services at Christmas, we find solace and peace,*

*A sacred space where love's wonders never cease.*


*A celebration of your birth, oh precious King,*

*In hymns and prayers, our voices joyfully sing.*

*We lift our hearts in worship and adoration,*

*Grateful for your love and divine revelation.*

*Church services at Christmas, a symbol of unity,*

*A gathering of believers, bound by faith's affinity.*

*In fellowship, we find strength and support,*

*A spiritual family, connected by a heavenly court.*

*The decorations within, a sight to behold,*

*Symbols of your birth, stories of old.*

*The nativity scene, a humble manger so dear,*

*Reminding us of your love, drawing us near.*

*Candles flicker, casting a warm and gentle glow,*

*A beacon of hope, your light in darkness does show.*

*The flame symbolizes your arrival, so divine,*

*Guiding us on a path of love, yours and mine.*


*Communion, a sacred act, we partake,*

*Bread and wine, symbols of your sacrifice we make.*

*In remembrance of your body and blood,*

*We find forgiveness, redemption in the flood.*

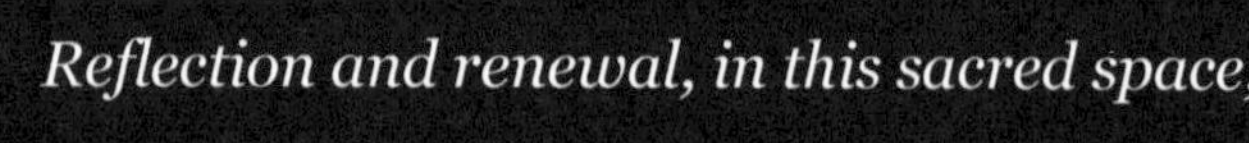

Reflection and renewal, in this sacred space,

We ponder your teachings, seeking your grace.

A time to repent, to realign our ways,

To follow you faithfully, all of our days.


Oh, King of kings, as we gather in your house,

May your presence surround us, like a gentle douse.

In church services at Christmas, we find your love,

A reminder of your birth, from heaven above.

*So, let us rejoice, as we come together,*

*In church services at Christmas, where love's tether,*

*Binds us as one, in worship and praise,*

*Oh, King of kings, our voices we raise..*

Record your observations.

# Ode 8.

# Reflecting on Acts of Kindness at Christmas

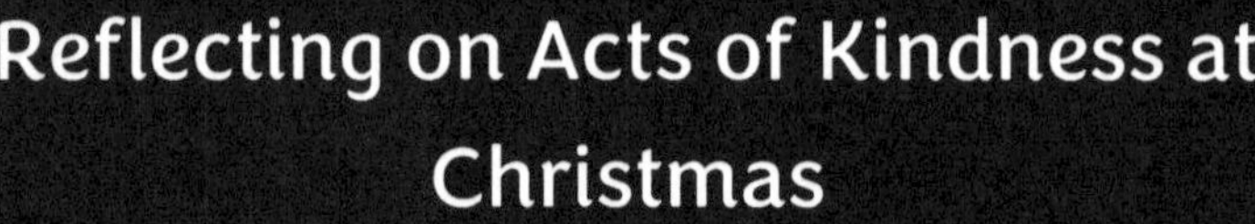

*Oh, King of love, in this season so bright,*

*We seek to emulate your kindness and light.*

*Through acts of compassion, we spread your grace,*

*In every smile and gesture, love finds its place.*


*Acts of kindness at Christmas, symbols so dear,*

*They embody the spirit that brings us near.*

*Love and compassion, they beautifully portray,*

*Reflecting the essence of your birth, we say.*

*Giving and generosity, a reflection of your heart,*

*We share our blessings, playing our part.*

*Like the Wise Men who brought gifts so rare,*

*We offer our love, showing others we care.*

*Hope and encouragement, in each act we bestow,*

*A glimmer of light in a world often shadowed so.*

*A kind word, a helping hand, a shoulder to lean,*

*Symbolizing the hope that Christmas has seen.*

*Unity and community, together we stand,*

*Bound by love, reaching out, hand in hand.*

*Acts of kindness unite us, breaking down walls,*

*In a world that so often divides and enthralls.*


*Joy and happiness, in each smile we share,*

*A ripple effect, spreading everywhere.*

*Kindness is contagious, it multiplies with glee,*

*Bringing joy to others, setting their spirits free.*

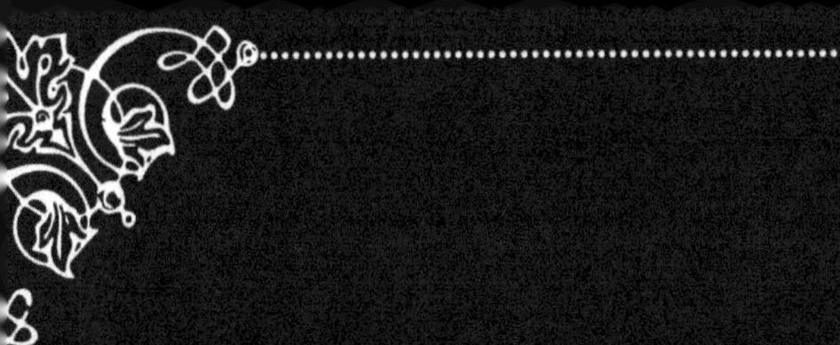

*Gratitude and appreciation, we express,*

*For the blessings we have, we are truly blessed.*

*By extending kindness, we give thanks anew,*

*Acknowledging the grace that flows through.*

*Renewal and transformation, in acts so small,*

*We become vessels of love, answering the call.*

*Kindness changes lives, it has the power to heal,*

*In giving, we find purpose, a deeper meaning revealed.*

*Oh, King of love, as we reflect on your birth,*

*May our acts of kindness bring joy to this earth.*

*In each gesture, may your light brightly shine,*

*Spreading love and compassion, a gift divine.*


*So, let us embrace the spirit of Christmas so bright,*

*Through acts of kindness, let us bring your light.*

*In every smile, every helping hand we extend,*

*May your love and grace, oh King, transcend.*

# Record your observations.

# Ode 9.

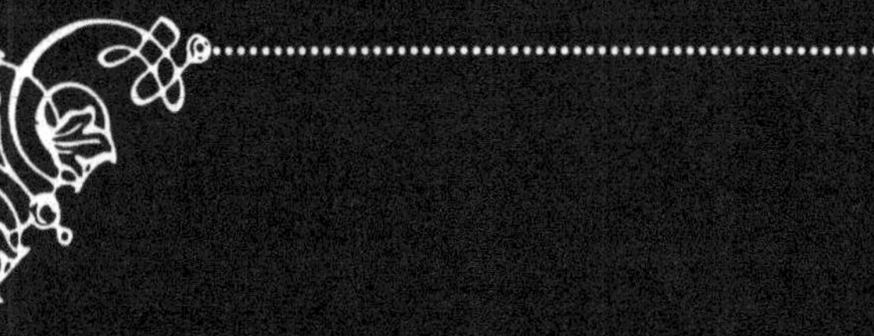

# Reflecting on Christmas Lights

*Oh, King of Light, in this season so bright,*

*We adorn our homes with radiant light.*

*Christmas lights, symbols of hope and cheer,*

*They illuminate the darkness, drawing us near.*


*Christmas lights, a triumph over the night,*

*A reminder that your love shines so bright.*

*In the midst of winter's cold embrace,*

*They bring warmth and joy to every place.*

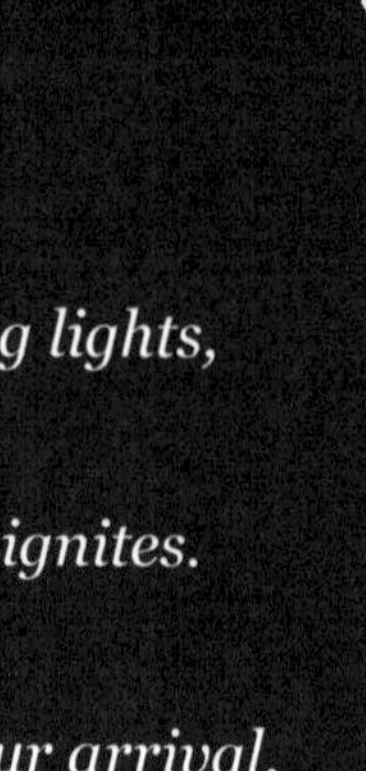

*Oh, King of Love, in these twinkling lights,*

*We see the beauty that your birth ignites.*

*They symbolize the celebration of your arrival,*

*The divine presence that brings revival.*

*Festivity and joy, they bring to our hearts,*

*As Christmas lights create a heavenlyl art.*

*With vibrant colors and sparkling glow,*

*They fill our souls with happiness, we know.*

*Christmas lights, a symbol of unity,*

*As communities join in festive serenity.*

*In decorating our streets, we come together,*

*Bound by love, in this season of togetherness, forever.*

*Guidance and direction, they softly impart,*

*Like a lighthouse, they illuminate the path of the heart.*

*They remind us to walk in love's embrace,*

*To follow your teachings, with kindness and grace.*

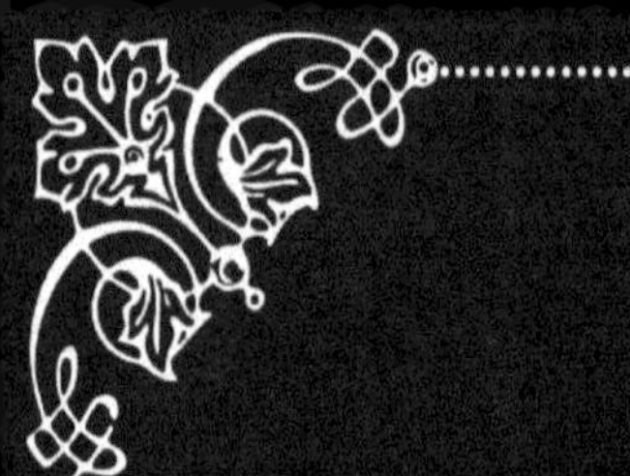

*Oh, King of Wonder, in these lights we find,*

*A sense of awe, captivating our mind.*

*They bring beauty to the world around,*

*A reminder to appreciate the wonders abound.*

*Faith and hope, they symbolize so true,*

*In the twinkling lights, we find strength anew.*

*Belief in miracles, blessings yet to come,*

*They inspire us to have faith, even when life feels undone.*

*Oh, King of Light, as we gaze upon the glow,*

*May your love and grace continue to flow.*

*In Christmas lights, may we see your presence near,*

*Guiding us through the darkness, dispelling fear.*

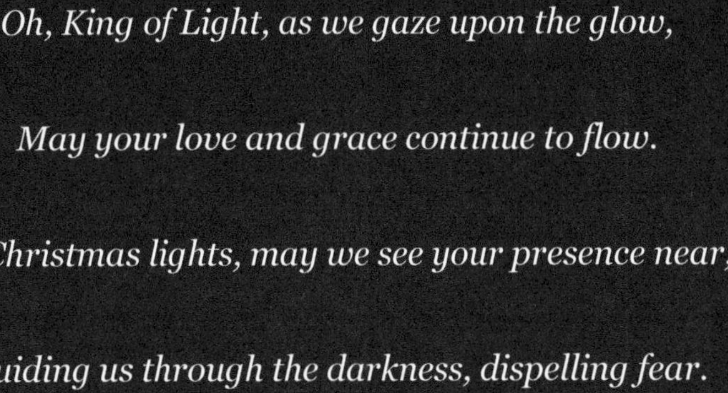

*So, let us rejoice in the symbolism they hold,*

*These Christmas lights, shining bright and bold.*

*In their glow, may we find your eternal embrace,*

*Oh, King of Light, filling our hearts with grace.*

# Ode 10.

# Reflecting on Peace and Goodwill at Christmas

*Oh, King of Peace, in this season so dear,*

*We gather together, spreading love and cheer.*

*Christmas, a time of reconciliation and grace,*

*Symbolizing the hope for peace in every place.*


*Peace, the essence of your birth,*

*Bringing harmony to a troubled earth.*

*In the manger, a symbol of humility,*

*You taught us the way to unity.*

*Oh, King of Forgiveness, in this time of reflection,*

*We seek to mend broken hearts with affection.*

*Christmas, a time to let go of strife,*

*Embracing forgiveness, restoring life.*

*Reconciliation, a gift we can bestow,*

*Healing wounds, letting compassion flow.*

*In the spirit of goodwill, we find unity,*

*Breaking down barriers, fostering community.*

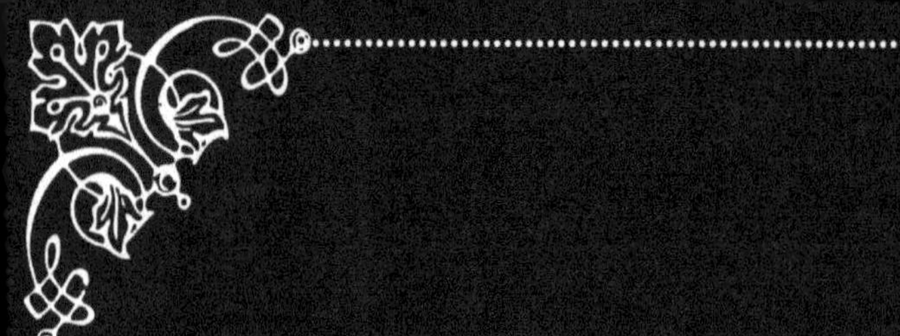

*Oh, King of Kindness, in this season of giving,*

*We extend love to all, in the way of living.*

*Christmas, a time for acts so grand,*

*Spreading joy and peace throughout the land.*

*Acts of kindness, a symbol of goodwill,*

*Bringing light to hearts, removing the chill.*

*From small gestures to deeds profound,*

*We share love, making hearts resound.*

*Oh, King of Global Peace, in this time of reflection,*

*We stand in solidarity, in every direction.*

*Christmas, a reminder of our shared humanity,*

*Working towards peace with unwavering tenacity.*

*Global peace, a vision we hold dear,*

*Extending compassion to those far and near.*

*In the spirit of goodwill, we unite,*

*Fighting injustice, eradicating plight.*

*Oh, King of Hope, in this season so bright,*

*We believe in a world where all is made right.*

*Christmas, a beacon of hope so true,*

*Inspiring us to create a better world, anew.*

*Hope for a better world, where peace prevails,*

*Where love and kindness never fails.*

*In the spirit of Christmas, we find our way,*

*Spreading hope, making a difference each day.*

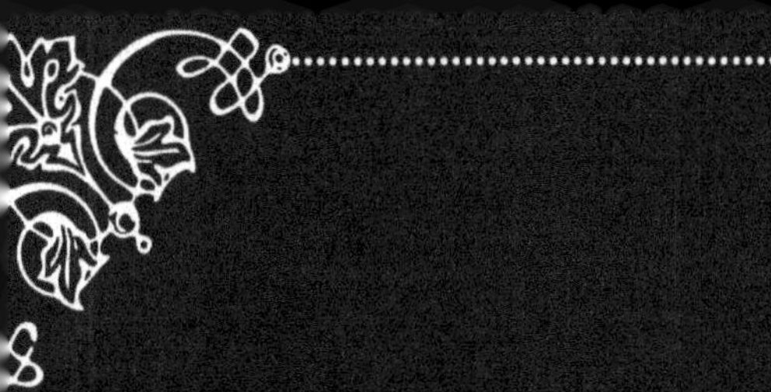

Oh, King of Reflection, in this time of renewal,

We examine our hearts, seeking to be truthful.

Christmas, a time to renew our commitment,

To embody peace, love, and goodwill, without limit.


Reflection and renewal, a path we take,

Examining our actions, the choices we make.

In the spirit of Christmas, we strive,

To live in peace, as long as we're alive.

So, let us embrace the symbolism so grand,

Of peace and goodwill, across the land.

In the spirit of Christmas, let love be our guide,

Spreading peace and goodwill, far and wide.

# Record your observations.

www.ingramcontent.com/pod-product-compliance
Lightning Source LLC
Chambersburg PA
CBHW040156160726
48006CB00014B/1774